ANIMAL BATTLES

# ORCHID MANTIS VS. ASIAN GIANT HORNET

BY NATHAN SOMMER

BELLWETHER MEDIA • MINNEAPOLIS, MN

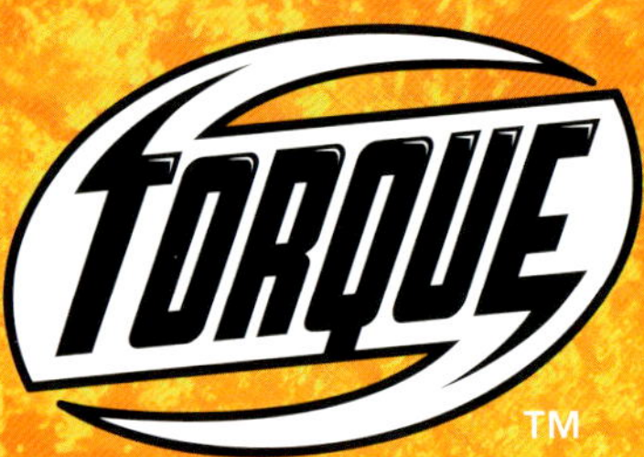

**Torque** brims with excitement perfect for thrill-seekers of all kinds. Discover daring survival skills, explore uncharted worlds, and marvel at mighty engines and extreme sports. In *Torque* books, anything can happen. Are you ready?

This edition first published in 2026 by Bellwether Media, Inc.



Library of Congress Cataloging-in-Publication Data

LC record for Orchid Mantis vs. Asian Giant Hornet available at: https://lccn.loc.gov/2025012853



Editor: Suzane Nguyen Designer: Josh Brink

Printed in the United States of America, North Mankato, MN.

# TABLE OF CONTENTS

THE COMPETITORS .................... 4
SECRET WEAPONS .................... 10
ATTACK MOVES .................... 16
READY, FIGHT! .................... 20
GLOSSARY .................... 22
TO LEARN MORE .................... 23
INDEX .................... 24

# THE COMPETITORS

The forests of Southeast Asia are home to many **insects**. Orchid mantises use their colors to hide in plain sight. They wait to attack **prey** at the right time.

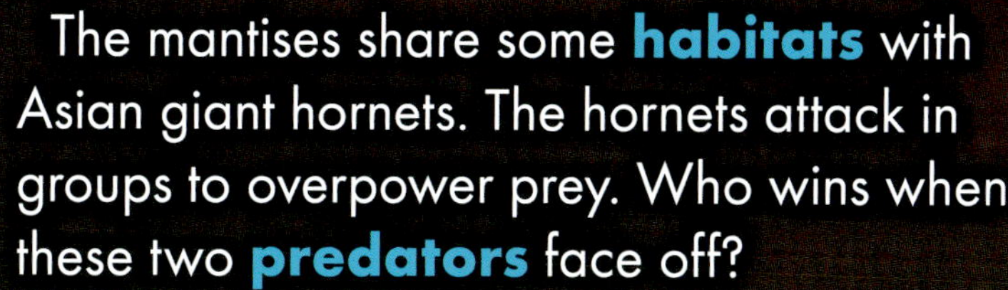

The mantises share some **habitats** with Asian giant hornets. The hornets attack in groups to overpower prey. Who wins when these two **predators** face off?

Orchid mantises have long, pinkish white bodies with two pairs of wings. They have large, pointy eyes. Their thin legs have **adapted** to look like flower petals.

Orchid mantises are found in the **rain forests** of Southeast Asia. They live in bushes and on trees. They hunt from flowers.

## DOUBLE TROUBLE

Female orchid mantises can be more than double the size of males!

# ORCHID MANTIS PROFILE

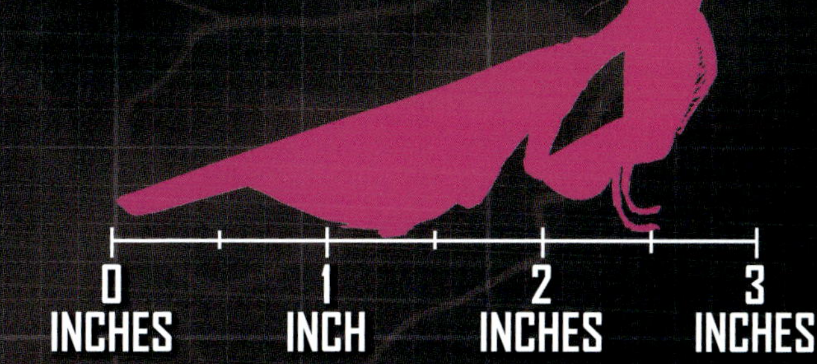


LENGTH

2.75 INCHES
(7 CENTIMETERS)

HABITAT

RAIN FORESTS

ORCHID MANTIS RANGE

# ASIAN GIANT HORNET PROFILE

LENGTH

2 INCHES
(5.1 CENTIMETERS)

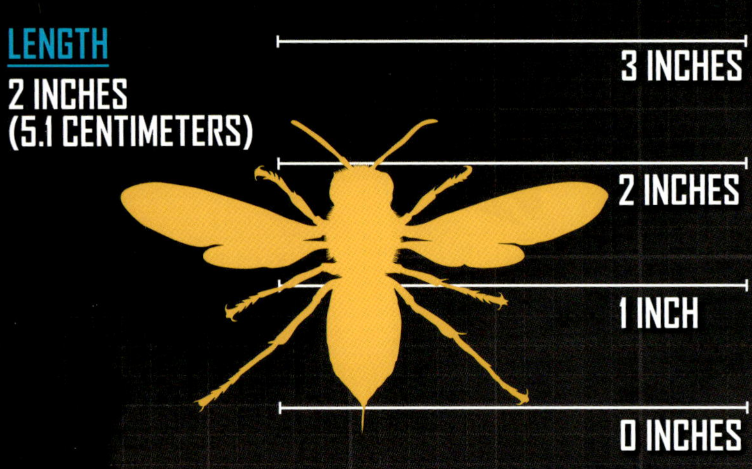


HABITATS

FORESTS

MOUNTAINS

ASIAN GIANT HORNET RANGE

Asian giant hornets are the world's largest hornets. They grow up to 2 inches (5.1 centimeters) long. Their wingspan can be up to 3 inches (7.6 centimeters) wide.

Asian giant hornets have wide, orange heads with large, dark eyes. Their thick bodies have black and yellow stripes. They are found in the forests of eastern and Southeast Asia.

## HORNET HOMES

Asian giant hornets often live in nests that are built underground.

# SECRET WEAPONS

Orchid mantises use **mimicry** to look like flowers. Their petal-shaped legs draw in hungry insects. The mantises quickly capture prey that comes too close!

# ASIAN GIANT HORNET STINGER SIZE

0 INCHES 1 INCH

0.25 INCHES (0.64 CENTIMETERS)

Asian giant hornets use stingers to give painful stings. These deliver **venom** into prey. The stings from the hornets can even be deadly to humans!

# ORCHID MANTIS GLIDING DISTANCE COMPARISON

Orchid mantises use their petal-shaped legs as wings. These help them escape from danger. The insects can glide up to 48 feet (14.6 meters) at once!

Asian giant hornets have sharp **mandibles**. They use these like scissors to remove the heads of bees. One hornet can defeat 40 bees in one minute!

# SECRET WEAPONS

ORCHID MANTIS

MIMICRY

WINGED LEGS

SHARP TEETH

Orchid mantises have sharp teeth. The mantises use these to bite the heads off some prey. Their teeth allow them to hunt prey up to three times their size.

Asian giant hornets use teamwork to take down prey. They can hunt in groups of up to 50 members. A group of hornets can defeat thousands of honeybees in hours!

# ATTACK MOVES

Orchid mantises mostly hunt other insects. Larger mantises can defeat frogs and mice. Females are even known to eat their own **mates**!

## HORNET DIET

**Asian giant hornets also eat nectar, spiders, and even other hornets!**

Asian giant hornets mainly hunt honeybees. **Solitary** attackers wait outside beehives. They attack bees as they enter and exit. Then they carry the bodies back to their nests for food.

Orchid mantises **ambush** their prey. They hide among flowers. Then they snatch prey out of the air with their legs! They eat the animals alive.

## SWAYING MANTISES

Orchid mantises sway back and forth. This makes them look like a flower being blown by the wind!

Asian giant hornet groups attack one beehive at a time. They fight until the entire hive is defeated. Even small groups can destroy hives within hours!

# READY, FIGHT!

An orchid mantis hides among flowers to catch prey. But the prey is an Asian giant hornet! The mantis bites the hornet.

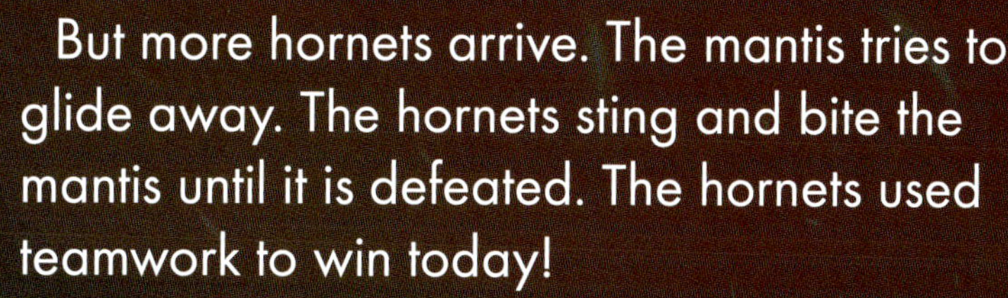

But more hornets arrive. The mantis tries to glide away. The hornets sting and bite the mantis until it is defeated. The hornets used teamwork to win today!

# GLOSSARY

**adapted**—changed over a long period of time

**ambush**—to carry out a surprise attack

**habitats**—the homes or areas where animals prefer to live

**insects**—small animals with six legs and hard outer bodies; an insect's body is divided into three parts.

**mandibles**—jaw-like body parts that some insects use for biting and cutting food

**mates**—partners

**mimicry**—adaptations that make one living thing look like another in order to better survive

**predators**—animals that hunt other animals for food

**prey**—animals that are hunted by other animals for food

**rain forests**—thick, green forests that receive a lot of rain

**solitary**—related to living or acting alone

**venom**—a kind of poison used to hurt or paralyze enemies

# TO LEARN MORE

## AT THE LIBRARY

Downs, Kieran. *Praying Mantis vs. Black Widow Spider.* Minneapolis, Minn.: Bellwether Media, 2022.

Gray, Susan H. *Murder Hornets Invade Honeybee Colonies.* Ann Arbor, Mich.: Cherry Lake Publishing Group, 2021.

Peterson, Megan Cooley. *Asian Giant Hornets.* Mankato, Minn.: Black Rabbit Books, 2024.

## ON THE WEB

**FACTSURFER**

Factsurfer.com gives you a safe, fun way to find more information.

1. Go to www.factsurfer.com
2. Enter "orchid mantis vs. Asian giant hornet" into the search box and click 🔍.
3. Select your book cover to see a list of related content.

# INDEX

adapted, 6
ambush, 18
attack, 4, 5, 17, 19
bite, 14, 20, 21
colors, 4, 6, 9
eyes, 6, 9
females, 6, 16
flowers, 6, 10, 18, 20
glide, 12, 21
groups, 5, 15, 19
habitats, 4, 5, 6, 7, 8, 9
hide, 4, 18, 20
hunt, 6, 14, 15, 16, 17
insects, 4, 10, 12, 16
legs, 6, 10, 12, 18
males, 6
mandibles, 13
mimicry, 10
nests, 9, 17
predators, 5
prey, 4, 5, 10, 11, 13, 14, 15, 16, 17, 18, 20
range, 4, 6, 7, 8, 9
size, 6, 7, 8, 9, 11, 14, 16
Southeast Asia, 4, 6, 9
stingers, 11, 21
teamwork, 15, 21
teeth, 14
venom, 11
weapons, 14, 15
wings, 6, 12

The images in this book are reproduced through the courtesy of: Opayaza12, front cover (orchid mantis), Yasunori Koide/ Wikimedia Commons, front cover (Asian giant hornet), p. 13; Kurit afshen, pp. 2-3, 4 (orchid mantis), 20-24 (orchid mantis); Satoshi Kuribayashi / Nature Production / Minden, pp. 2-3, 17, 19, 20-24 (flying forward hornet); kororokerokero/ Getty, pp. 2-3, 20-24; Fufill, pp. 2-3, 20-24; photolife95/ AdobeStock, p. 5 (top Asian giant hornet); Hiroshi_K/ AdobeStock, pp. 5 (bottom Asian giant hornet), 8-9; lessysebastian/ AdobeStock, pp. 6-7; Eric Isselee, p. 7 (orchid mantis vector); Green Wall Std, p. 8 (hornet vector); Pong Wira, p. 10; Ken Ishigaki/ Wikimedia Commons, p. 11; Phil Degginger/ Alamy, pp. 11 (stinger), 13 (mandibles), 15 (stinger, sharp mandibles), kuritafsheen/ Alamy, pp. 12, 14 (winged legs); Eko Budi Utomo, p. 14 (mimicry); Ais Qocak, p. 14 (sharp teeth); Alen thien, p. 14; EDU Vision/ Alamy, p. 15 (teamwork); Mark MacEwen/ Alamy, p. 15; monster_code, p. 16; Masayu Andrini, p. 18.